T is for TREE

A BIBLE ABC

Connie L. Meyer

REFORMED FREE PUBLISHING ASSOCIATION

© 2018 Reformed Free Publishing Association

All rights reserved

Printed in the United States of America

The scriptures cited are taken from the King James (Authorized) Version.

Reformed Free Publishing Association
1894 Georgetown Center Drive
Jenison, Michigan 49428
rfpa.org
mail@rfpa.org
616-457-5970

Written and illustrated by Connie L. Meyer
Cover design by Erika Kiel and Connie L. Meyer
Interior design and typesetting by Katherine Lloyd, The DESK

ISBN: 978-1-944555-27-6
LCCN: 2018930299

To all children of the Reformation,

children who live by faith,

faith in the promises of God

"For therein is the righteousness of God
revealed from faith to faith: as it is written,
The just shall live by faith."

—ROMANS 1:17

A is for ANTS

Though weak and small in size,

They gather food all summer.

May God make us as wise.

"There be four things which are little upon the earth,
but they are exceeding wise: the ants are a people not strong,
yet they prepare their meat in the summer."

—PROVERBS 30:24–25

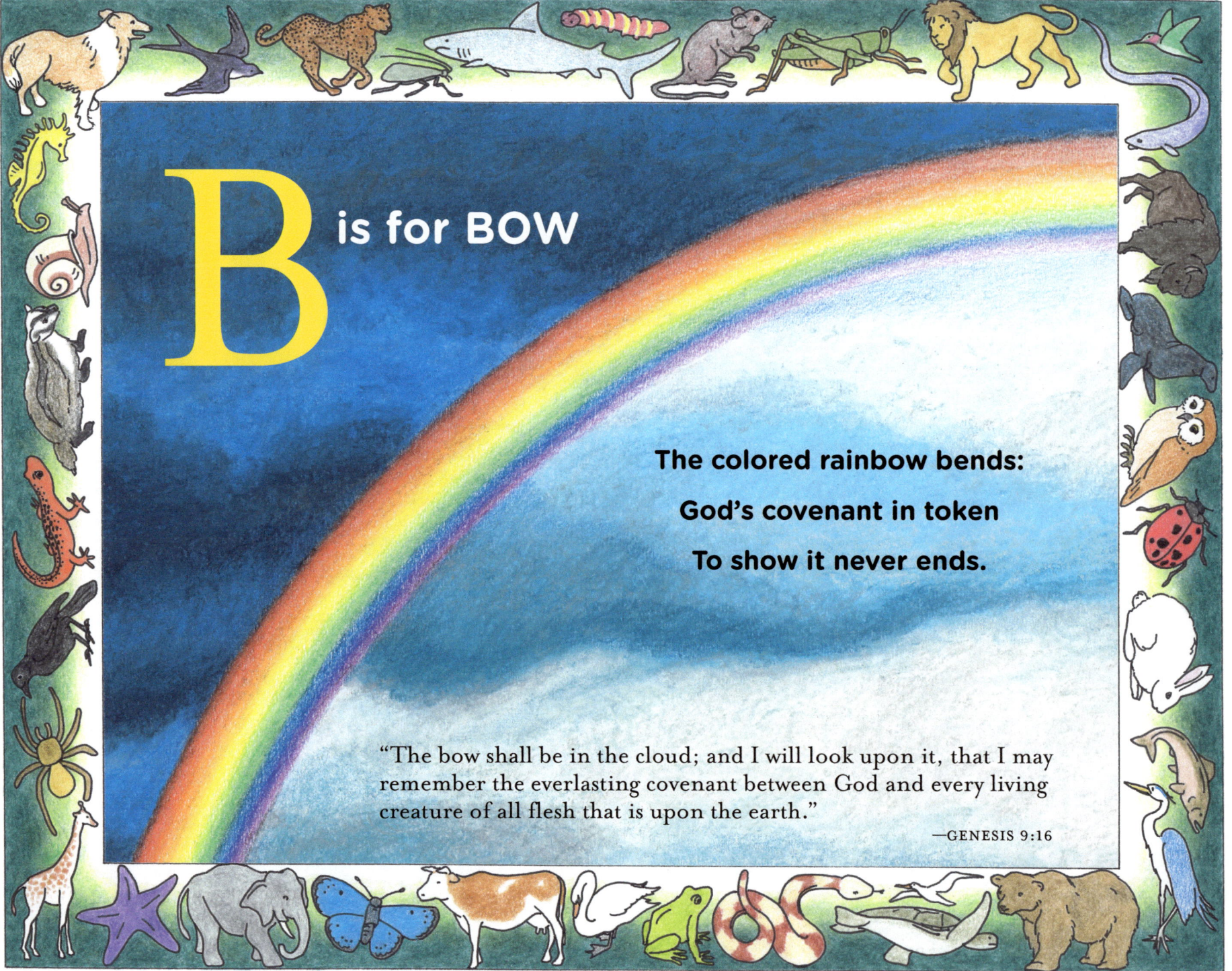

B is for BOW

The colored rainbow bends:

God's covenant in token

To show it never ends.

"The bow shall be in the cloud; and I will look upon it, that I may remember the everlasting covenant between God and every living creature of all flesh that is upon the earth."

—GENESIS 9:16

C is for CLOUDS

They tower up so tall.

We sing of God's great mercy

That's higher than them all!

"Thy mercy is great above the heavens: and thy truth reacheth unto the clouds."

—PSALM 108:4

D is for DAWN

When morning lights the skies.

Our Savior is the day star

Who in our hearts will rise.

"We have also a more sure word of prophecy; whereunto ye do well that ye take heed, as unto a light that shineth in a dark place, until the day dawn, and the day star arise in your hearts."

—2 PETER 1:19

E is for EAR

To hear what's wise and true;

Like seeking hidden treasure

Found only by a few.

"My son, if thou wilt receive my words, and hide my commandments with thee;
so that thou incline thine ear unto wisdom…and searchest for her as for hid treasures;
then shalt thou understand the fear of the LORD, and find the knowledge of God."

—PROVERBS 2:1–2, 4–5

F is for FAITH

A mighty gift of grace;
As little as a mustard seed
Will move a mountain's place!

"If ye have faith as a grain of mustard seed, ye shall say unto this mountain, Remove hence to yonder place; and it shall remove; and nothing shall be impossible unto you."

—MATTHEW 17:20

G is for GOAT

The scapegoat was the one

Sent out into the wilderness

To picture Christ the Son.

"The goat, on which the lot fell to be the scapegoat, shall be presented alive before the LORD, to make an atonement with him, and to let him go for a scapegoat into the wilderness."

—LEVITICUS 16:10

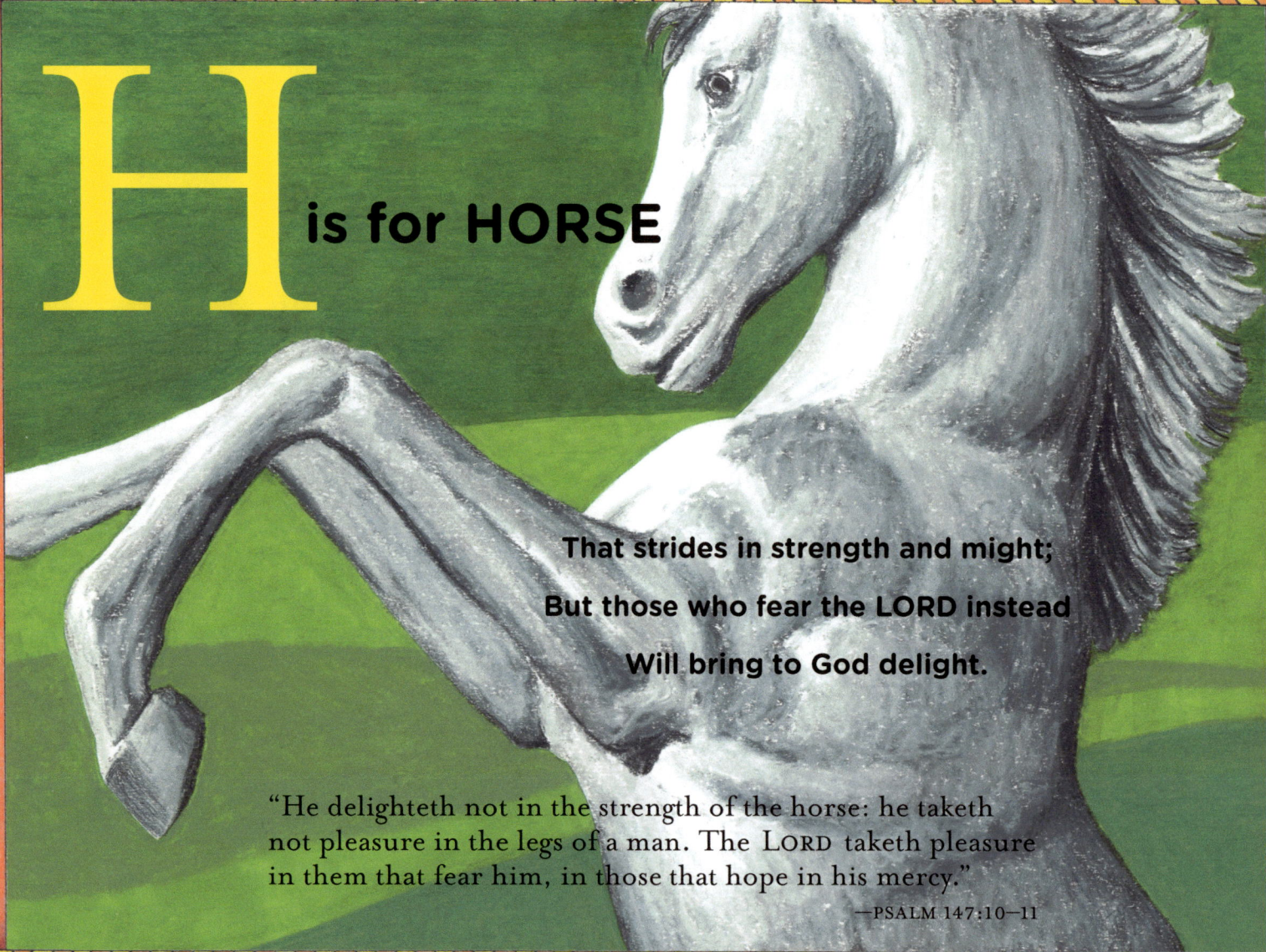

H is for HORSE

That strides in strength and might;

But those who fear the LORD instead

Will bring to God delight.

"He delighteth not in the strength of the horse: he taketh not pleasure in the legs of a man. The LORD taketh pleasure in them that fear him, in those that hope in his mercy."

—PSALM 147:10—11

I is for ICE

Cast out across the land.

Our God sends forth his bitter cold.

Before it, who can stand?

"He casteth forth his ice
like morsels: who can
stand before his cold?"

—PSALM 147:17

Receive my instruction, and not silver; and knowledge rather than choice gold. For wisdom is better than rubies; and all the things that may be desired are not to be compared to it.

J is for JEWEL

There's rubies, and there's gold;

But far more precious are the lips

That speak with knowledge told.

"There is gold, and a multitude of rubies: but the lips of knowledge are a precious jewel."

—PROVERBS 20:15

K is for KING

The ruler of a land.
Directed like a river,
His heart is in God's hand.

"The king's heart is in the hand of the LORD, as the rivers of water: he turneth it whithersoever he will."
—PROVERBS 21:1

L is for LEOPARD

A fearsome cat of prey;
But in God's new creation,
A child will lead his way.

"The wolf…shall dwell with the lamb, and the leopard shall lie down with the kid…and a little child shall lead them."

—ISAIAH 11:6

M is for MOON

A natural law of light.

To show God keeps his promises,

It shines on time each night.

"Thus saith the LORD, which giveth the sun for a light by day, and the ordinances of the moon and of the stars for a light by night, which divideth the sea when the waves thereof roar...if those ordinances depart from before me, saith the LORD, then the seed of Israel also shall cease from being a nation before me for ever."

—JEREMIAH 31:35—36

N is for NEST

A swallow built her nest
beside God's holy altars.
Oh, there I long to rest!

"My soul longeth, yea, even fainteth for the courts of the LORD…Yea, the sparrow hath found an house, and the swallow a nest for herself, where she may lay her young, even thine altars, O LORD of hosts, my King, and my God."

—PSALM 84:2–3

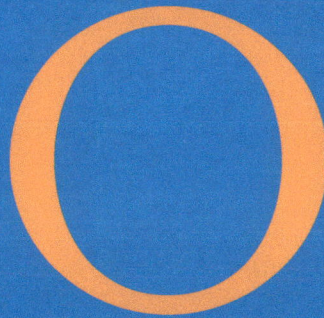

O **is for OLIVE**

A plant of precious worth;

A picture of God's children dear

Who fear the LORD with mirth.

"Blessed is every one that feareth the LORD…happy shalt thou be, and it shall be well with thee. Thy wife shall be as a fruitful vine by the sides of thine house: thy children like olive plants round about thy table. Behold, that thus shall the man be blessed that feareth the LORD."

—PSALM 128:1–4

P is for PATHS

On paths that we must take,
We pray for God to lead us
In truth for his name's sake.

"Shew me thy ways, O LORD; teach me thy paths. Lead me in thy truth, and teach me: for thou art the God of my salvation."
—PSALM 25:4–5

Athanasian Creed ...but one eternal...
...not three eternals...
Heidelberg Catechism ...both in life and death, am not my own...
Canons of Dordrecht is the fountain...
...Election...
Apostles' Creed ...I believe in God...
Belgic Confession of Faith ...We all believe...
Creed of Chalcedon We, then, following the holy fathers...
Nicene Creed God of God; Light of Light, true God of true God...
And in one Lord Jesus Christ...

Q is for QUAILS

When Israel had complained,

"We want some meat!" then God sent wind

And quails upon them rained.

"And there went forth a wind from the LORD, and brought quails from the sea, and let them fall by the camp, as it were a day's journey on this side, and as it were a day's journey on the other side, round about the camp."

—NUMBERS 11:31

R is for RAVENS

They sow not, yet they eat.

If God provides for birds like them,

Our needs he'll surely meet.

"Consider the ravens: for they neither sow nor reap…and God feedeth them: how much more are ye better than the fowls?"

—LUKE 12:24

S is for STARS

Their number who can tell?
By this God showed to Abraham
His seed would be as well.

"[God] brought [Abraham] forth abroad, and said, Look now toward heaven; and tell the stars, if thou be able to number them: and [God] said unto him, So shall thy seed be."
—GENESIS 15:5

T is for TREE

That grows where waters flow,

With leaves that never wither;

A blessed man is so.

"Blessed is the man...[whose] delight is in the law of the LORD...And he shall be like a tree planted by the rivers of water, that bringeth forth his fruit in his season; his leaf also shall not wither; and whatsoever he doeth shall prosper."

—PSALM 1:1–3

U is for UNDER

Like chicks beneath a wing,

We're under God's protection;

In trust, to him we cling.

"He shall cover thee with his feathers, and under his wings shalt thou trust: his truth shall be thy shield and buckler."

—PSALM 91:4

V is for VINE

From which grows fruit and limb;
A picture Jesus gave that shows
How we abide in him.

"I am the vine, ye are the branches: He that abideth in me, and I in him, the same bringeth forth much fruit: for without me ye can do nothing."

—JOHN 15:5

W is for WINGS

Spread wide as eagles soar,

Like those who wait on God will grow

In grace and strength the more.

"They that wait upon the LORD shall renew their strength; they shall mount up with wings as eagles; they shall run, and not be weary; and they shall walk, and not faint."

—ISAIAH 40:31

X is in FOXES

In holes they have a bed;

But for us Jesus suffered this:

No place to lay his head.

"Jesus saith…, The foxes have holes, and the birds of the air have nests; but the Son of man hath not where to lay his head."

—MATTHEW 8:20

Y is for YOKE

On oxen pulling weight.

"Come unto me," said Jesus;

On us his yoke's not great.

"Come unto me, all ye that labour and are heavy laden, and I will give you rest. Take my yoke upon you…For my yoke is easy, and my burden is light."

—MATTHEW 11:28–30

Z is for ZION

God's dwelling place of old.

He'll soon bring us to heaven

Where streets are purest gold.

"Judah shall dwell for ever,
and Jerusalem from generation
to generation…For the LORD
dwelleth in Zion."
—JOEL 3:20—21

"The street of the city
was pure gold, as it were
transparent glass."
—REVELATION 21:21

Connie L. Meyer has written and illustrated extensively for children. She is the author and illustrator of *Behold the Beauty*, a three-volume Christian art curriculum series for children in kindergarten through sixth grade; *Gottschalk: Servant of God*, the story of a medieval monk who stood firmly for the truth; and more than 175 short stories for the "Little Lights" page of the youth magazine *Beacon Lights*. Connie has also written articles in the *Standard Bearer* magazine under the rubric "When Thou Sittest in Thine House," copyedited and illustrated Bible stories for the Protestant Reformed Sunday School Association, co-authored a junior high art curriculum for the Protestant Reformed Teacher Education Development Committee, and volunteered in a Christian school as a reading tutor for first and second graders.

Connie is a 1982 graduate of Calvin College and holds a BA in art education. She is also a wife, mother, and grandmother. Connie and her husband Neil live in Grand Rapids, Michigan and attend Hope Protestant Reformed Church.

www.ingramcontent.com/pod-product-compliance
Lightning Source LLC
Chambersburg PA
CBHW040713150426

42813CB00061B/2983